Short Stories: Reflections of My Life Encounters

Jacqueline McNeil-Henry

Copyright © 2021 Jacqueline McNeil-Henry

All rights reserved. No part of this book may be reproduced in any form or by any electronic or mechanical means, including information storage and retrieval systems, without permission in writing from the publisher, except by reviewers, who may quote brief passages in a review.

ISBN: 978-1-955312-21-9

Printed in the United States of America
Story Corner Publishing & Consulting, Inc.
1510 Atlanta Ave.
Portsmouth, VA 23704

Storycornerpublishing@yahoo.com
www.StoryCornerPublishing.com

Dedication

I am grateful, first to God, for giving me the desire, time, and talents to undertake such a project.

I dedicate this book of my life's encounters to the loves of my life, my children, family, & friends.

Acknowledgments

I want to acknowledge a few special people in my life. I know I do not have time or the page space to list you all, but I know you all are dear to my heart.

To my mother, the late Frances Myers McNeil, who was the world to me. She taught me to appreciate education and how to be an independent and responsible daughter. She also taught me how to love and trust God through everything.

To my father, the late William Lawrence McNeil, who was also my world. He left his kind and humble spirit imprinted on my heart. He showed me how to be kind and loving to everybody despite their actions.

To my son, Rashid Tyrone Henry, who is my heartbeat. You are a very respectful young man who makes me immensely proud. You always show me love, and I am forever grateful.

To my beloved daughter, Shatyra Blondell Henry, who is also my heartbeat. Shay, you have encouraged me over the past few years to write a children's book. I had no desire to write any books, but here it is, Shay. Perhaps the children's book will come later. Thank you for everything. I appreciate your trust and faith in me.

To my sweet and only grandchild, Jalen Rashid Henry. What can I say? Mom-mom loves you to infinity.

I want to send my appreciation to all my siblings, aunts and uncles, cousins, church families, and my circle of solid friends for lifting me up throughout the years.

I want to give special recognition to my special cousin, Grenita Smith-Hall, for sharing Story Corner Publishing & Consulting, Inc.'s information and encouraging me to produce this edition.

And finally, to my devoted furry daughter, Angel Pearl Harris-Henry, who went home to Glory and left me missing you. Rest easy baby (June 12, 2005 to April 13, 2021 @ 6:00 pm).

Table of Contents

Introduction

Story 1: The Seeds of Life

Story 2: Who Am I?

Story 3: The Other Side of Darkness

Story 4: The Joys of Parenting

Story 5: My Latch-Key Son

Story 6: The Facets of My Divorce

Story 7: My Little Curly Locks Baby Girl

Story 8: Living The Dream of My Family's Culture

Story 9: Can You Sing? Yes, You Can!

Story 10: Selling Made Easy

Story 11: Generating Funds From A Dime

Story 12: Whatcha Talking About?

Story 13: How to Age Gracefully and Successfully

Story 14: My Dad's Transitioning Journey

Story 15: The Sting of Death

Story 16: My Mama – A Virtuous Woman

Introduction

Completing this project gave me purpose as to what to do during this stage of my life, retirement. Even though I have been deemed a creative and gifted writer by several of my college professors, I never imagined that I would pull my ideas and life encounters together to produce a published book.

In sharing my knowledge through this book production, I desire to enhance your life and educational experiences by introducing or redirecting you to the following principles:

- How to compare the human life cycle to the life cycle of nature.
- How to practice using "please and thank you" to make a difference in how you are perceived.
- The fundamentals of living and surviving among racially and discriminatory barriers.
- The benefits of training, disciplining, and encouraging children so they can become respectful adults.
- The successes of letting young children take on greater responsibilities.
- How to live happily and successfully beyond divorce.
- How to love adopted children as your own.
- The techniques of how to mingle with other cultures and nationalities.
- The techniques of singing in greater octaves.
- The methods of effective fundraising and selling.
- How to speak up and out with motivational confidence.
- How to live healthy with hereditary conditions.
- The principles of accepting death and dying of loved ones.
- How to deal with the processes of grief.
- The principles of a virtuous woman.

This compilation of principles may not suit everyone, but I hope a few lessons will be learned. I have experienced each principle I have referenced in some manner and have found that life is more extraordinary for me because of the differences they have made in my life.

The Seeds of Life

◊ ◊ ◊ ◊ ◊ ◊

Using my imagination and reflecting back to 1948, a seed was planted through moments of pleasure by my parents in the rolling hills of Pamplico, South Carolina. As a result of the implanting and cultivating of that seed, it grew and grew until it was ready to "peep" out into the world and blossom.

After being released into the world, it was fed, watered, and given warmth with the best care. It grew and grew very tall, firm, and upright. It became a small tree. Each time its limbs drooped or withered, they were propped back up and given more nutrients, water, warmth, and care.

As this special care was given, this tree grew and grew, stronger and stronger. As its roots begin to spread lengthwise, it took on some of the strength from the earth. As its color deepened, it became a beauty to observe as it stood swaying in the gentle breezes.

Years began to pass by, and this young tree began to grow older and firmer. It did not sway much anymore because of its deeply planted roots and strong foundation.

Small children used its dangling limbs to climb upon and play. Older teens leaned against it to embrace their lovers and carve hearts with names into its thickened walls. Others used it as landmarks to obtain directions. However, it was used or abused, this tree continued to hold its place.

Soon this tree grew so tall that its limbs hung down from the top from the weight it carried. The upper branches began to thin out and lean whenever strong winds lingered for any length of time.

As this tree began to lean downward and sway in the gentle breezes, its branches caught onto another tree and entwined itself into its branches and leaves. Soon these two trees became as one and formed an even more shady spot as they stood locked together.

After many years, these two trees continued to stand together. They had branched out far and wide. One day a new branch sprouted out from beneath one of the trees and grew into the same coloring of the original tree. I can imagine that this was their offspring because it formed the same patterns in its growth and development.

As this new birthed younger tree grew taller and broader, its strength quickly began to make the original tree lean and sway because of the weakness in its roots.

After much continued growth by the younger tree, the branches of the older tree began to break away piece by piece and soon dissolved into the earth from whence it came.

Life starts in perfect harmony for some of us and ends in such a sad state of aloneness. Even though the seed was planted in pleasure and grew with warmth and loving care, it soon lost its vitality and eventually died a slow and lonely death. It was no longer used for its actual purpose. It slowly crumbled back into the earth alone, without any children, teens, or pleasure.

Life is truly short – only given to us for a short time to make the absolute best out of it. Go ahead, sow your seed and live!

Who Am I?

◊ ◊ ◊ ◊ ◊ ◊

I am a small, petite person in stature with a huge heart. My motto has always been to never look down upon a person unless I'm lending a helping hand to pick them up. Many folks commence to stepping on people when they are down and out or going through a storm of life, when in fact, to lend a helping hand would present little effort. I have always felt that people need people most during times such as these.

I could easily be labeled a people person, for my love for people stretches far and wide. I love to aid others – not for the glory and honor it usually brings, but because it is deeply rooted within my soul.

I find myself being called upon many times to help people accomplish and resolve many of the everyday problems that everyone, at some point in their life, has or will face. Many of my friends or associates often ask me to make introductions to members of the opposite sex. Many elderly folks ask for my assistance or advice in helping them to make life choices in benefits provided by social agencies. Aside from giving this advice, I often assist them in processing the necessary forms and in obtaining the required verifications for such. I have also been called upon to recommend job opportunities for friends and relatives and other resources. During my career, I have hired or made available job opportunities for many. These are just a few examples of how I show my love and concern for all people and not for compensation, glory, or honor.

People give respect when they get respect. Respect is such a small word that means such a great deal to others. If an adult shows respect to a child by allowing them to be heard, that child will listen to the adult in return. If a man respects his wife and treats her like a lady, she will generally respect him and treat him like a man. If a pastor shows respect to his congregants, they in turn, will respect him and his ministry. Teachers giving respect to students will gain the same respect. So, in essence, people usually give what they get. I always try hard to respect others, even though this is a small task for me because this is an integral part of my nature. Two of the most undesirable things I detest are to see a child disrespecting their parents or another adult and to see a woman or man disrespecting each other. This is even more unsavory when it is done in public view.

Some other small words with significant meanings are thank you and please. These words, again, come naturally for me and, when they are used, can make all the difference in the world. I have been able to get many stubborn children to perform specific tasks merely by saying please. During my working career, I have gotten many of my staff members to perform additional tasks by saying please and thank you. These words show a sign of concern and appreciation for whatever is asked to be done.

So, you see, some small things carry lots of weight. It may be a tiny task to help someone do what they feel is the impossible, such as reading directions or correspondence for someone whose eyes are failing, but they will appreciate your help and remember you for it. When a child trips and falls and gets up crying from skinned knees, they will usually stop crying and feel much better if someone provides a little comfort and love to them.

Who am I? I am a small person in stature, with a big heart. I am a small person who sometimes uses small words to tiny people and gets tremendous results, respect, love, and appreciation.

This is who I am.

The Other Side of Darkness

◊ ◊ ◊ ◊ ◊ ◊

The title of this manuscript, The Other Side of Darkness, seems most appropriate during these times, with all the discussions regarding the racial divides and "Black lives Matter" protests ongoing in America.

Some people of other cultures and environments appear not to be aware of some of the struggles and prejudices we, as black people, or people in the minority sectors, have faced throughout our lives. We look upon this division of societies as a natural birth because it has been evident for so many years, and frankly, some of us have grown accustomed to this way of life and seek no refuge. They have been unfortunate enough to have been raised with the idea deeply implanted that if you are not white you take the back seat automatically without question or resentment. In other words, this is your place.

Many of us, even though raised under this same charter, have rebelled against society, and gone on to prove that skin color, in no way, depicts the intelligence or secures any markings for any human being. Some have gone over and beyond set boundaries to become outstanding dignitaries and have succeeded, but still have not been entirely accepted into the social circles of the "other world," as I call it.

It is true that there are many people who are still not aware of all the prejudices we have faced and presently are facing in this society, merely because of the color of our skin. But, as we grow, we become more aware of our existence and surroundings and eventually begin to recognize the differences.

As a Black person, no matter which direction you choose to climb or how long you climb when you reach the top, there will always be another mountain. I therefore, always try to pack a little extra in my "backpack" when I start on my journeys, and when I reach my other mountain, I reach in my backpack and fill it up with what it takes to continue climbing my other mountain. This way, and only this way, will we ever reach the top in a society such as we continue to live in today, just like yesterday.

The Joys of Parenting:
Step-Parenting, Single-Parenting, and Adoptive Parenting

◇ ◇ ◇ ◇ ◇ ◇

A parent is the father and mother of a child. The father of a family or the mother, if they are the legal guardians, should support the children and educate them. Today, many laws provide for and dictate the duties and responsibilities of the parent. In most states, if the parents fail to provide food, clothing, and shelter for their children, they are held responsible for any debts the children accumulate for these items. Parents may correct and punish their children when necessary, but parents may be penalized if they are cruel and are abusive to their children resulting in afflicting injury. The state may take a child away from the guardianship of their parent if such action is warranted for the child's welfare.

As the parent of a natural child, stepmother to an older child, adoptive mother to a child, and a single parent to each of them, I have tried hard to be a responsible parent and raise responsible children. There are many systematic ways of dealing with family relationships and problems. Functioning as a parent can be the most exciting and rewarding part of life, especially if you are blessed to have great children such as I have. Regardless of whether some parents are performing as expected, their children can still cause some unwanted difficulties. Again, I am blessed not to face these woes. Even though we long to have good children, we often do not know how to train them. Most parents agree that the ideal child should have what is called the four R's. The first "R" is respect. The child should be considerate of other's feelings, should treat others fairly, and not permit others to mistreat them. Children become respectful when treated respectfully. Parents have a responsibility to respect children likewise. Parents should give them some freedom of action, consider their wishes, grant them independence, and not regard them as property. A loving parent can damage their children through disrespectful behavior. A parent can be a successful guide for their children's development if they understand the goals of their children's behavior. The second "R" is responsibility. The children should contribute to the family's well-being, be helpful in the home, do chores without being reminded, participate willingly in family life, and not act as if they have a servant. Children become responsible by being given responsibilities.

The third "R" is resourcefulness. The children should be capable of taking care of themselves, should be able to entertain themselves, possess the ability to meet new people and new situations, and should be independent and self-reliant. Children become resourceful if they are permitted to take stabs at solving some of their life's problems. The fourth "R" is responsiveness. The children should be friendly, affectionate and they should like adults and enjoy being with them. They should enjoy life. They receive love and should reach out to give love to others. Children become responsive when treated relatively with love and respect.

Angry, rebellious, uncooperative, hostile, or vengeful children are usually due to a lack of parental know-how. Many parents do not know how to handle their jobs and do not understand their children. They do not understand human behavior. They have incorrect concepts about discipline and training.

A child adapts to members of their family. Through their experiences, they discover which actions succeed and which one fails. Children desire to belong. A wise parent understands that a child operates to improve their status while responding to the needs of others because they wish to belong. A wise parent allows the child sufficient room to develop without letting him infringe upon the rights of others.

Most parents try to be authoritarian by saying things such as, "you do what I say or else." But in today's environment, the child often rebels and will do what the parents wish, only under compulsion. More and more children refuse to obey rules regardless of the severity of punishment. That often angers the parents and sometimes results in a battered child syndrome, in which the child gets beaten harshly and sometimes is hospitalized. That can be avoided by not being so assertive but giving each other mutual respect. Parents, too often, overprotect a child and shelter them from valuable experiences.

Parents should have confidence in children. Being over fearful is harmful to them. Parents should stop pampering and spoiling children. That is also harmful. It gives children an incorrect view of life and makes them dependent and demanding. Parents often overestimate their children by thinking they are the best and usually expect them to get preferred treatment. Many parents over-supervise and smother their children, which is harmful. They believe they should always know what the children are doing.

Many parents believe the best way to train a child is to reward them for good behavior and punish them for wrong. That is not necessarily true. That can shape a child's behavior and development with some undesired effects such as untruthfulness, sneakiness and makes the children unsure of themselves. Parents should always try to first obtain voluntary cooperation from their children by encouragement, being cooperative, and using non-authoritarian procedures. If this fails, parents should fall back on the method widely known as natural and logical consequences.

A discouraged person is usually convinced that he is not as adequate as others and often gives up without even trying. Parents easily see their child's weak points. They should try hard also to find their strong points. When a child does poorly, they need more encouragement than when he does well.

Being a stepparent, natural parent, adoptive parent, and single parent, I feel that I have experienced and learned the many ways to raise the kind of children one would be proud of and the kind of child that eventually will be proud of their children. There are different fundamentals of parenting. Sometimes using psychological means is the tool to utilize to obtain the consequences necessary for independence to be developed in some children.

I thank God for giving me the ability to raise intelligent, confident, and loving children.

My Latch-Key Son

◊ ◊ ◊ ◊ ◊ ◊

Latch-key children are youngsters nationwide between the ages of five and thirteen, who at some time of the day, before school, after school, or in the evening are regularly un-supervised by someone over fourteen.

My son was the product of a latch-key kid. I had planned for my son to be dropped off at the sitter's home during after-school hours, which happened to be right next door to my parent's home. Therefore, many days my son would spend time with my parents after completing his homework. My procedures were to pick him up, drop in to see my mother, who had become the caretaker for my dad, who had suffered a stroke, and we would ride home together and share in his activities of the day.

One day my son expressed that he no longer wanted to go to the sitter and that he was old enough to come home and use his reference books to complete his homework. I decided to give in to his request since I knew sooner or later this would happen anyway. I therefore, reluctantly, informed my next-door neighbor that he would be coming home after school and asked if she would keep an eye on him since she was home all day. I explained to him and my neighbor that once he was in the house, he was to call me at work immediately. He was not permitted to open the door for anyone and could not go out until I came home. I instructed my secretary to let me know immediately if my son did not place the "I am home" call if I was in a meeting or away from my desk. Thank God he complied. Additionally, I gave my neighbor the key to my home just in case my son lost his key during school hours. This arrangement went smoothly except for the times when he lost his keys from the chain he carried around his neck, which occurred often. Since my son was not the disobedient type, I did not have to worry about him breaking the house rules regarding turning on appliances. He diligently called me every day before 4:00 pm and then prepared to do his homework. Since I knew he was home alone, I made every effort to come straight home and go back out with him if necessary. As a single parent, it worked out fine for me.

Years ago, many educators assumed that most latch-key children came primarily from minority groups and low-income, single-parent homes, in which the parents could not afford stable child-care arrangements. That is not necessarily true and was not true in my circumstances, for the caring of my child was my absolute priority.

During this era, Federal studies offered Census Bureau data reflecting that most of these children are white, middle class, and live in suburban or rural communities. Most of these children are ten-thirteen years old. There are fewer latch-key children than had been previously stated, according to Dr. Hofferth, a Health Science Administrator, and their characteristics are substantially different.

Other studies have shown that parents are more likely to leave children alone if they are more independent, live in better neighborhoods, or if the children are older. Many critics called the studies untrue and said it is inaccurate because there is a great deal of under-reporting. Some parents are ashamed and guilty and do not want to admit it, plus it is illegal in some states for children to be left alone in this manner.

Many critics found it hard to believe that this is a middle-class, white suburban problem because there was not enough money to support school-age programs for low-income children. Many felt that the best way to get truthful answers was to ask the youngsters about their care arrangements. Studies performed with interviews from 2,000 children estimated that more than a fourth of all elementary school children were left alone four or five days a week for two hours or more. Many professionals that work with others have said that latch-key children are not predominantly low-income or predominantly middle-class.

Talking to many working parents, they feel that after-school care is a real problem. Parents think that if their children were in someone's care, it would provide them with more peace of mind. They recognize that most children are frightened of being home alone.

The method that I used for my son was extraordinarily successful. If specific values are instilled in children and they are made to be responsible and obey the home rules, the situation would work itself out for all concerned.

Please note that my son is a grown adult now and being a latch-key kid proved to be a rewarding experience for him and me. Please also note that several of the studies cited in this writing have changed over the years. Additionally, this millennium generation of children feels that a child staying home alone is the "norm" because many of these parents today are children raising children and are unaware of the possibility of unfavorable results that could occur while these children are alone.

The Facets of My Divorce

◊ ◊ ◊ ◊ ◊ ◊

Even though divorce is quite common today, it is still listed as one of the most emotional and up-setting life crises a person can ever go through.

I have gone through a divorce, but the period of my separation, before the divorce had the most impact on my life. I was left to think of all the changes I had to make and all the problems I would face. I was lonely for adult companionship even though I had several friends and family. I knew that I had to provide for the upbringing of my young son. I was angry at the fact that he had to grow up in this single home environment. Of course, I blamed the entire ordeal on my husband. (Not really)

I had a sound financial foundation and a good sense of direction, but still, I felt left out in my family circle, only because I had led what I thought was the ideal and near-perfect life. While the separation and divorce were a choice that I had made, I guess I was angry for having been put in a position to make such a decision.

I feel that even though the aftermath of a divorce may be an isolated time in which you might want to be alone, you can still gain tremendous growth from this crisis. Most people I have conversed with, who have gone through a divorce, feel that they have made great strides since the divorce. Today's marriages can be very disappointing to many people. Many people who share happy marriages do not often experience as much growth in their relationships as single persons fighting to regain control of their lives. Studies show that those women who are the most happily married are those who are the most submissive and the least able to be assertive. When marriage is an essential part of a woman's life, her desire for personal identity is often curtailed because of the demands placed on her by her spouse and children. The single woman has many more options for pursuing a new, meaningful personal identity and becoming more of her own woman.

One of the things that I learned during the separation from my husband was the advice given to me by my attorney, family, and friends. Some of the advice I was able to implement and some of it I just accepted and used at my discretion. However, I would advise anyone separating, before divorce proceedings, to seek legal advice from an attorney. The more factual information you can get, the more prepared you will be in the long run. When choosing an attorney, it is crucial to choose one whom you like and trust. It is essential to choose one who is experienced in matrimonial law. It is quite possible to seek and receive all legal fees acquired during the divorce proceedings from the opposing spouse and one-half to one-third of the income. I would also advise keeping a financial diary of all expenses. This will verify and substantiate the salary and other income. If child support or alimony is required during the interim period of separation and divorce, you can go to court and petition for these funds from your spouse. I would also suggest any woman dealing with a divorce should prohibit going to an attorney, being naïve, and putting her life in their hands. Prepare yourself, learn as much as you can, and do not be too trusting. Many lawyers often push ridiculously hard for a divorce and often do not consider the possibility of reconciliation. They usually want to wrap up your case as soon as possible to obtain their fees and do not give you all the needed information. Women should also be aware of attorneys who make propositions to them. That is bad business, and they should not become involved. Attorneys sometimes will take advantage of these situations.

I have found that after being married to a man and having had his children, you still have feelings after the divorce. Just because you want them to go away, they often do not unless the divorce was messy and abusive. Caring feelings for an ex-spouse is a stage that practically every woman I have spoken to has experienced. Time does heal, perhaps not completely, but to some degree. You must be incredibly careful, however, of these feelings during this time and make sure they are real if you are considering reconciling. Many times, these are feelings of loneliness, the need for security, or for the children's sake. You should try to be honest with yourself and analyze whether you truly still love your spouse and want to make another go of marriage with them. It would be best to consider whether changes have been made for betterment or whether it is because you feel guilty.

All divorced parents probably feel that they have failed their children by breaking the marital bond. That again is guilt. If you let guilt get in the way, it will deprive you of any comfort, satisfaction, or pleasure you can get from those who sincerely care about your well-being. Children can play on your guilt also. You should be aware. Instead of feeling guilty, take the attitude that you did the best you could in your marriage and that you are doing your best now. Take a positive approach. It is often difficult to control your anger and bitterness, but I have found that no matter how angry you are, it is best not to degrade your spouse to your children. They love their parent and will hate you later for doing this. My children have been my salvation. As they get older, I get more pleasure from them and thank God for them every day. God provided me with everything I needed during the most challenging period in my life. He has been my "rock" and a companion to me during good and bad times. He has been my all and all, and He has never left me alone. He promised to bear my burdens and give me peace, and He did.

Some women who have children at home have a hard time beginning to date. Some feel that the children will think she is immoral if she does. They believe that they should only see their mother with one man, and that would be their father. However, you cannot stop living because of your children, and it may be that they resent your dating because you feel ashamed of it. I do recommend, however, sitting down and talking to your children regarding it, but do not let them control your life.

The loneliness of a divorced woman is different from any other kind. That is because she must rebuild her entire life and face living alone. She must get used to meeting new people, in addition to coping with finances and children's concerns. But I have learned that I have control over my loneliness and can do things to make myself feel better on days when I am tired of being alone. A particularly good friend always told me that,

"It is up to you to make yourself happy," and it is so true. I will never forget him for this statement.

First dates can be difficult. It is a situation that does not easily bring comfort or relaxation. I have found that to make dates as pleasant as possible is to avoid talking about your troubles, your divorce, or your children's problems or concerns. If your date brings up these topics, say, "I am out to have a good time, and when we get to know each other better, we can discuss these topics." If you are not sure what to talk about, sports are an easy topic.

I do not know if I will ever re-marry. If I do not, I know that I can still be happy because I have built a satisfying lifestyle. Every divorced woman can reach this stage in their life if they keep working toward this growth goal. To know where you are going, it is helpful to know where you have been. I have found more strength within myself than I ever dreamt that I had. I have grown because of my experiences, some of which have been painful and disappointing.

Learning to live as a single woman can be both exciting and rewarding. I have become more outgoing, more confident, and more assured of who I am and what I desire. I have made many wonderful new friends from both sexes and have enjoyed seeing my children develop and grow most positively and pleasingly. I have become more self-sufficient, resourceful, creative, positive, and bask in knowing that I like myself even more than I did during my marriage.

Today, as I look at my life, I have no regrets. Even the painful experiences have taught me something about myself and others. I have found that the only way to enjoy life as a single woman is to accept that you are single. I have begun to live my life now and not as if it is a "waiting game" to be re-married. Further, I do not look upon my marriage as a failure but as a courageous step I made to become a "whole person." Divorce gives you the opportunity for a new and better life. But you, the single woman, must make this happen. What I have learned, most importantly, is that I can accept myself for who I am today and that I know that I will continue living for the real me for the remainder of my life.

My Little Curly Locks Baby Girl

◇ ◇ ◇ ◇ ◇ ◇

As I grew up, I had a special love for children, especially little girls. I often dreamed of having one of my own to be able to cuddle her in my arms, kiss her good night and gently lay her down to sleep.

I always admired the "prissiness" they displayed, even as a toddler. They always seemed to capture everyone's heart with their cuteness, bouncy and playful behaviors. If their parent desired to ensure that they were "dressed to kill," as I would be, their closets would be filled to the brim with lacey dresses, slips, socks, ribbons, and hair ornaments.

I recall, as a child growing up, how I "primped" and "platted" the hair of my neighbor's children, changing their hairstyles time after time. I also admired their starched petty coats that made their little dresses stand out afar from their little legs. Their ribbons and bows matched their outfits exactly.

I always wished for a little girl when I had children of my own. Unfortunately, nature did not see it this way. When I did get married and had my first child, I was blessed with a handsome son that was 8lb, 13oz, and 21in long. I was never happier than when I laid my eyes on him and, especially when I opened his tiny "balled up fists," counted his fingers, and they were all there. My son grew up to be a handsome little guy, "the apple of my eye," who captured his mother's heart. He acted more like my little brother than my son because of the relationship we developed into maturity.

Even though many years had passed since my son was born, I still longed to be able to cuddle a little girl and to engage in the purchasing of the frilly dresses. With this growing desire, I eventually sought to fulfill my needs by contacting several adoptive agencies since my marriage was no longer viable. Many of my friends and family members tried talking me out of pursuing this agenda, but I was destined to follow my heart by fulfilling this desire. I knew that even being a single mom, God would not put more on me than I could handle.

To move forward, I made the application, completed my home study, attended several weeks of workshop training, received my approved financial status, criminal, and background checks, and waited to be matched with this little angel.

As the day came to bring this tiny angel home, it was another one of the happiest days of my life. I was able to cuddle her, kiss her and lay her gently down to sleep. I thank God for the welcoming blessings of this child, whom I adore.

Living The Dream of My Family's Culture

◊ ◊ ◊ ◊ ◊ ◊

Based upon my black, southern cultures, my definition of a family structure consists of a relationship between a man and a woman, which often results in the bearing of children, their siblings, parents, and in-laws from both sides of the family and any cousins that are generated between the first and third generations. Because of this widespread of relatives, you see, a family could consist of quite a few members. Through my religious upbringing, I have learned how to establish a church family. This family is entirely different, but some of them often provide the same love and care that usually exist in families structured by birth and marriage.

Society has described families as an institution of humans that will survive or disintegrate based on whether family life is weak or strong. Through studying, I have learned that families have existed since the earliest times and will exist if man lives on earth. Families are the basis of society's needs and the continuation of the human race.

I have observed many family members and have concluded that their cultures and lifestyles have allowed them to sometimes survive in a non-caring world. They have had to lean whole-heartedly on their relatives to help them make all the difference. Had their families not been there for them, they most likely, would certainly not have been productive to society. Furthermore, they would not have even made it through infancy. Many relatives have had to extend their roles by looking after and caring for children born into their family structures.

In my family, as we were nurtured, cared for, and raised, we were also taught the values of life, the mechanism for survival, and how to manage our daily living to become responsible and successful adults. As a result of these teachings, I grew up to become a responsible adult and have learned the basic needs and values of our human race. I knew that you must contribute something worthy to get worthiness out of life.

During my upbringing, my parents made our home the center of all activities. That meant that the meals were prepared and served at the appropriate mealtimes of the day. Dinner was always the main event because of the conflicting schedules of each of us throughout the day. At this meal, we would all come together, grace the table with our thanks, eat and discuss the day's happenings. I have experienced, in my family settings, that this sets an excellent atmosphere for expressing your concerns for family members and their daily activities. This is also a great time to express ideas from a group's perspective and share good quality time. This, too, will help families to communicate better and stay in touch with each other.

My father always stood, unwavering, as head of our household. He was indeed the breadwinner. My mother, however, stood right beside him. Her stance helped him to become a successful man. Where he may have been limited somehow, she was strong, and he accepted this fact. Within our household, each of my siblings was assigned daily chores to perform. We were required to rotate these chores, such as washing dishes and cleaning the kitchen, so everyone would have a chance to handle each duty. By assignment of these tasks, it helped us to realize the responsibility and how to integrate better.

After establishing my own family, I began to analyze specific pointers. I recognized that certain values and traits instilled and placed upon children would remain with them as adults, whether positively or negatively. I also realized that the organization of the family structure influences a good, sound home environment. Society has designated man as the authority figure, but he must prove his worthiness to remain in this powerful position. I have experienced that if one family member tries to rule or dominate the other and is allowed to do so, respect is lost and extremely hard to regain. I find it best to share ideas in all instances. Children should also be permitted to suggest or express their opinions, but the parents or adults should usually make the final decisions.

Can You Sing? Yes, You Can!

◊ ◊ ◊ ◊ ◊ ◊

Singing is the act of producing music with the human voice. Singing has always been one of my favorite hobbies. Singing to me is as much of a natural function of the human voice as speaking. We speak, for most purposes, to relay our thoughts. We usually sing for joy during our early childhood but often express ourselves later through the lyrics and learn to show emotions in what we sing.

I began singing at a young age with my family members, at my church, and with several choirs that I joined. Singing has always been amazingly easy for me, so I am usually asked to perform the lead parts on most songs. My father, his family members, and friends sung in professional quartet groups, so I feel that my desire and love for singing was inherited.

I continued singing throughout my childhood with various family members. We formed groups and held regular rehearsals to enhance our voices for competitions in multiple contests and concerts. During these times, I found myself placing each participant on the proper notes, sometimes by singing their notes with them and eventually dropping out, leaving them to continue. I have never had a problem with voice ranges, so this task was easy for me to do with any note necessary to make the desired harmony. I would have each person singing songs repeatedly until the harmony would ring in tone. My siblings would sometimes become agitated with me for driving them so hard to obtain a professional sound, but when we completed a song, they agreed that it was much worth the effort. We soon realized what notes were required of us and could look at each other and feel where to fit in voice-wise. We established permanent voice ranges within the groups for each member. Therefore, the usual problems did not exist with staying on individual notes. We were sharp as a dime.

After high school, I joined an already established rock and roll group, which required me to travel extensively and record on several occasions. I would sing and entertain by night and work by day. On weekends, I traveled locally, throughout Pennsylvania, and through several cities of Canada. Although the name of my group changed frequently, the original singers generally remained the same. Our managers and musicians changed often, but we held fast to our mission of sticking together. However, when necessary and for reasons beyond our control, we removed or added new singers. I was always required to provide the proper training, protocols, and techniques to the new singers. For many artists, I was hired to perform background singing for recordings at Sigma Sound Studio and others in Philadelphia. I was paid for each session. However, I now understand that I should be collecting royalties from each recording. This musical and recording business leaves a lot to be desired, especially if you are unaware of the processes.

One of my trade names was the Sequinettes. The last trade name I sung under was the Equations, which consisted of three girls, Claudia, Tiny, and me. We performed each weekend and eventually recorded two selections. When our manager gave the master of this recording to an incredibly famous and well-known radio personality to market and play, he claimed that the master was destroyed accidentally. When consulting with the writer and producer of the recording, he concurred, citing the same story. Because we had put so much time and effort into recording these two selections, we were highly disappointed and finally gave up. However, some 10-15 years later, in 2014, a good friend of mine, who was aware of our trade name and the problems we had with our master being destroyed, located our "A" side recording which was listed on a compilation album being played in the UK. A short briefing regarding the recording stated that the song was recorded by a "Philly" group who should have made it. We were able to get copies of the recording and sought to go legal to prosecute the wrongdoers. Unfortunately, the radio personality was deceased, and the writer and producer had just died less than six months earlier. The other two singers and I discussed hiring an entertainment attorney to go after obtaining any monies due to the group, but to date, the process has not been pursued. I didn't want to follow the matter but was happy to have my voice on a copy of the CD to play whenever I needed to. I am not sure what the future holds for this endeavor. Only God knows since so much time has elapsed.

Fortunately for me, I never gave up singing and directing the church choirs. After the aftermaths of our recording and the hardships it brought the group, I got married. I gave up singing rock and roll professionally. I must admit that I had loads of fun while singing and traveling. I never stopped singing for my pleasure, and until this day, I still sing with enjoyment.

I accepted the position of President of the Resurrection Baptist Church, #2 Choir, and remained the president for several years. I also accepted the role of supervisor of the Youth Department, which required me to become more involved with my church and its activities. My responsibilities were to monitor voices, teach songs, to interpret lyrics, and arrange songs to obtain variations of sound for our Sunday morning worship services. My time was divided between both choirs as well as our family group, The McNeil gospel singers.

During this period, I began taking piano lessons, which enabled me to develop a better sound for each singing group. My piano music teacher taught me voice theory to be more successful in my teachings. Her providing and sharing these techniques gave me a better understanding of the processes. When we want to sing, nerves near the brain causes the vocal cords to vibrate to make the sounds audible. I was also taught that the average untrained voice can sing twelve notes, which covers the ranges of most famous songs, but well-trained voices can cover two octaves or sixteen notes. Some unusual voices, after much training, can cover three octaves. I taught my youth members, some who ranged from ages three to twenty-one, that these voices are classified by their range and tone color. I taught both groups that the highest woman voice is the soprano. Below this voice is the mezzo-soprano and following this the contra-alto. The highest male voice is the tenor, then the baritone, and below it is the bass.

The differences in natural voice quality and training types make it impossible to define their exact ranges. During my study, I found that most people can be taught to sing simple melodies. With the help of microphones, talented singers have made successful careers with voices of average power and ranges. However, to become an opera star or a concert recitalist requires a voice of unusual power, range, and quality. Some arias include extraordinarily high and low notes. This singer may have to sing many words without taking a breath. The training of the voice for professional singing takes patience and practice. A voice student must practice discipline in the way they stand, the posture of their body, the depth and ease of their air intake, and the relaxation of their neck and upper chest. Ranges of notes can be regulated by using the muscles of the lower chest and upper abdomen. A singer must learn to express human feelings. They should not neglect the study of music because the voice, at its best, is indeed a beautiful musical instrument.

During my musical studies, I learned that sheet music could indicate how and when to sing. Printed notations on the sheets can inform you of when the voice tone changes. "Pianissimo" means very softly, "fortissimo" means very loud, and "legato" means to sing smoothly. I had to learn the various chords, notes, timing, and pedals of the piano and provided these instructions to my children, who also took piano lessons. My voice warm-ups would begin by singing the scales using pure vowels. After this, I would switch to the words and phrases and finally to the entire song. I learned that singing clear and precise vowels and connecting them with light consonants improved enunciation. The principal requisites in singing are a good voice, a correct ear, and a sound knowledge of music.

My endless love for music has kept me actively striving to produce perfection in untrained ears and cultivating voice ranges by developing quality notes that have indeed led to a more brilliant and sweeter sound. This method has truly been rewarding for me. I think God for my voice and the opportunities to use it to please all people during many occasions such as worship services, funerals, weddings, reunions, and just in my shower each day.

I am truly blessed to be the mother of a daughter, Shatyra, who has mockingbird experiences in singing with ranges that I have never been able to reach. She is a wonder to behold and is going places, reaching greater heights... Watch out world!

Selling Made Easy

◊ ◊ ◊ ◊ ◊ ◊

A positive attitude and skills are the keys to the development of effective selling. Selling should be fun and exciting. You should enjoy it much the same way you do with some other favorite pastime. Selling is also a professional job with many principles, methods, and skills.

I have had the opportunity of working as a Sales Counselor with many different companies. I was responsible for selling old familiar products such as Copper Craft, Amway, Wicker, Home Decor products, and Sarah Coventry jewelry. During this process, I needed to define methods to increase my sales, ultimately increasing my dollars. I therefore, attended as many training sessions, sales rallies, and conferences as I could to assist me in obtaining a better understanding of the techniques to this professional skill. At these training sessions, one of the most important things that I learned was that employers often hire new salespersons with positive attitudes over those with more education, experience, or previous selling skills.

Selling can be a success or failure. It depends upon you. A person can succeed in selling if they learn and then practice accepted sales techniques, listen to their prospects, know the products they are selling, manage their time, and set priorities.

Some examples of failures in selling are when one depends entirely upon their personalities, comes on too strong with lots of pressure, does not respect the profession, is more interested in their commissions than their prospects, and refuses to learn from their mistakes. Generally, the difference between a professional and a non-professional salesperson is sensitivity, sincerity, attitude, and selling skills. All these factors can be achieved to make you a professional salesperson.

In addition to a higher income, becoming a professional salesperson can do many personal things for you. Interacting with some customers can bring more excitement than working a routine job. Selling can bring out the best in your personality. Those who become excellent at selling can often very quickly double their income. There are lots of common personality traits found in successful salespersons. They are usually self-starters, are persistent, like people, are energetic, are problem solvers, are good communicators, are ambitious, like money, enjoy recognition, and are not easily frustrated. Salespersons keep the channels of trade open, help to solve client problems and contribute in many other ways to society. Your image plays a significant part in creating the first impression to customers, so they must adhere to good grooming habits.

Salespersons, sometimes, must use psychological tools to become more successful. They should make customers feel good about themselves, expect to be turned down now and then, acknowledge that they do not have all the answers if that is the case, turn disappointments into an advantage, do not assume a sale is always going to be, and should prepare a daily plan of action.

It would be best to start on a positive course with customers by portraying a warm smile, making solid eye contact, and engaging in good posture. You should help the customer to relax and act more like an advisor rather than a person selling a product by trying to satisfy the customer's needs. Another sales technique to use is the rule of "three." If you can present different versions of the same product, limit the variety to three. More than three products will confuse. You can then close the sale by asking the customer which one they would prefer.

It would help if you learned all that you can about the product and the services it can provide. Ask the customers for their opinions and show respect. Give presentations, encourage questions, and answer them honestly, introduce financial arrangements and remain positive.

A good salesperson should not make promises to customers that they cannot keep. They should radiate confidence in themselves and their products. They should not criticize or condemn competitors. They should learn something from every lost sale, should not become discouraged and give up, should have a desire to please, should know that closing a deal is the most challenging part of selling, should use their time wisely, should set upward goals, should remain polite, should display good manners and plan to meet the world.

Finally, a good salesperson should always follow up with some form of a thank you to the customer, whether the sale is made or not.

Generating Funds From A Dime

◊ ◊ ◊ ◊ ◊ ◊

Regardless of the economic situation, if you belong to a club, board, non-profit, or for-profit organization, one of the first things to be discussed is the need to raise funds. Sometimes the need is more significant than others, depending upon what limits have been established. Funds are sometimes donated to offset expenses, but most of the time, people do not have the extra funds to give, so they turn to fund-raising. Raising funds for communities or other activities can be fun and easy with a bit of planning and working together. Once the necessary funds are obtained, it seems to revive the spirits of the organization.

As the parent of two children, who were highly active in a variety of activities, I have been involved in fund-raisers, of all types, for several years. For most of these activities, I held leadership or chairperson roles, so I had direct dealing and was instrumental in ensuring that funds were sought and received. To procure some of these funds, I have led rallies, organized sales of dinners, bus trips, candy and cookie sales, pen and pencil sales, light bulbs sales, first-aid kits sales, boat rides, pantry parties, chances for drawings, tables for bazaars, stationery sales, shopping sprees and many other types of activities, too numerous to list.

My success formulas have all been based upon the way you start each project. I always start with the premise that the job would not be easy and with no guarantee that it will be successful. The next step is to begin the planning process, which will detail the time and efforts others are willing to spend to bring money into the organization.

The chairperson or leader selected for the project is probably one of the most important decisions you will have to make. This person can either make or break the fund-raiser. They must be reliable, energetic, interested in the specific cause, and get along with those who will also be working on the project. If you are working for a youth organization, you should secure the assistance of their parents or other adult leaders. They will be critical to the fund-raising success. When making assignments during the project, it is essential to let people volunteer and make their choices, if possible, of how they would like to proceed. People will rebel if given too many orders and, therefore, will not function at their best. Especially in dealing with children, this procedure almost always works. They will present less resentment, even if it is an unwanted assignment, if they have been allowed to make a choice. You would be treating them in an adult manner, and they will respond as such. Remember this, especially if it is their organization where you are raising funds.

If fund-raisers should warrant younger children going to stranger's homes, they must be accompanied by an adult or have them make regular phone check-ins to assure others of their safety. Money for fund-raisers is essential, but the safety of the children is more important.

The next step is to select a date for the event. You must ensure that it is convenient and does not conflict or involve any competition from other events. If the event is to be held outdoors, a rain date should be selected. I try to steer clear of having events on holidays but rather keep them on Saturdays or Sundays. There can never be too much planning done, but it should be done carefully, making lists and checklists of completions. At your first meeting, share your list of ideas with others to receive some additional ideas you may have missed, forgotten, or never thought to do. You need to think about the budget, equipment, advertising, and people support. You must discuss and analyze what resources you already have, what you can borrow or rent, the legal aspects of the project, its safety, and just how each step will be accomplished.

You should set a goal. That should be based upon your need unless the fund-raiser is generally to build your treasure. In this case, you should decide how much money will be spent to fund the anticipated project and determine if it is worth the expenses to do so. Cash already on hand is sometimes wiser to keep than taking the chances of using it and making lesser money in return.

If the location of the fund-raiser may create a problem for others, you should check with Municipal Officials to ensure that no laws or ordinances are being broken, such as a possible street bazaar that will prevent or interfere with the flow of traffic. In many instances, I have had to get permission to use a vacant schoolyard for our annual bazaar during off-school hours. This permit must be obtained in advance of the event. Any applicable taxes or fees must be paid in advance, as well as any contracts signed. If you are selling a product or a service from another person's firm, you may need a contract. Be careful not to sign any contracts that require you to pay in advance for any goods that may not be sold.

If you are offering children's rides and games to the public, make sure that the operators and firms are reputable in the use of their equipment and that they are appropriately insured. Some fund-raisers may need some security, as with a boat ride that I engaged in sponsoring annually that included alcoholic beverages. Other security needs may be for lost children or unruly persons causing disturbances. If convenient, it is an excellent practice to have a nurse or someone available to administer first-aid for minor injuries.

It is a good practice to select someone to oversee publicity, supplies, clean up, and to count and safeguard funds collected. All records regarding the event should be saved for future reference and reporting. They represent the blueprint also for future, successful projects. It would be best if you took the time to thank those who assisted you and especially those from outside of the organization. Make sure to pay all debts and identify who will need to sell certain items. For example, boys will not want to sell Girl Scout cookies. You should assign these tasks according to the member's talents and do not forget to allow them to make a few decisions of their own. This will help them to become future leaders while engaging in a learning process.

These helpful ways to organize fund-raisers have been used on different occasions and with diverse audiences. They have almost always helped me to reach our project goals successfully.

Whatcha Talking About?

◊ ◊ ◊ ◊ ◊ ◊

As we all know, a public speaker speaks publicly to people about a chosen topic and is usually expected to go about this speech realistically and effectively. I have had the opportunity to speak publicly on many occasions and have learned different ways to capture my audiences to deliver clear, concise, and meaningful speeches. I have been continually active in several auxiliaries, wherein, on several occasions, I have had to introduce and present speakers. That required me to acknowledge their past experiences, and I have had to prepare the audience to give their undivided attention to what was to be said.

God gifted me with the ability to sing, so I have had the privilege of belonging to family groups, rock groups, and various church choirs. I have sung background with many recording artists and have performed as a soloist. During many of these reflective moments, I was required to sing the lead on most songs. While singing with my rock groups, I was often called upon to entertain the audiences during band breaks and intermissions. I was often confronted with very cold and staring audiences, but I knew that I had to become creative and devise a way to get them engaged. That is not an easy task, but you cannot lose your audience.

I have narrated and have had acting roles in many plays and have served as Mistress of Ceremonies for many functions. Each time I had to concentrate on performing to the audience at hand. Each occasion may be different, and you must recognize this. On the employment scene, as manager, I held weekly staff meetings and was requested to lecture at various departmental meetings. Each time I was required to deliver speeches on various topics. Some were for disciplinary actions, staff re-organizations, changes in policies and procedures, and updates in health and welfare benefits packages. I have been selected to participate in panels of discussions, wherein I had to speak for specified periods and on given topics. As chairperson for the City of Philadelphia Employee's Combined Campaign, I had the pleasure of marketing and narrating a CD of the services provided by each member organization. This

CD was distributed to every city department to "kick-off" their giving. This was the works of one of my proudest moments.

While performing as a public speaker, to be effective, you must know the purpose of your speech and the interest and attitude of the people to whom you are speaking. This information can help you in selecting a topic, to formulate the speech, to choose supporting materials, and to choose the appropriate language to use.

I have found that persons who speak fluently in an effective manner are most likely to be leaders of some sort, and those who allow others to do all the talking are most likely to be followers. Training in effective public speaking is essential for maintaining leadership positions. A speaker is effective if, when trying to make information transparent, the audience understands the facts. If a speaker tries to persuade audience members to agree to something or change their opinion and is successful, it is an excellent example of effectiveness.

The four points every speaker must consider when preparing to make a speech is the subject, the audience, you as a speaker, and the occasion. A speaker can usually make a more effective presentation with a topic he has direct experience with, rather than a subject from someone else's experiences. Your subject matter should be appealing to the listeners. They should be divided into three essential types: those which inform, persuade, and entertain.

During most of my public speaking, I realized that when talking about subjects, in terms of my knowledge, without considering my audience, my speeches were ineffective. From these negative experiences, I have learned to try to determine what the audience already knows about the subject and if they want to hear more about the subject. I have also realized that people tend to listen only when they think the speaker's ideas will benefit them. It is always helpful to know more about the subject than you plan to share with the audience. My personality has always played an essential part in influencing my audiences.

A great speaker, I feel, should think very carefully about the time and place of his speech. He should decide if the occasion is appropriate for the subject chosen. After careful thought is given to the matter, the audience, personality, and the event, the speech should then be planned. The first step in planning a speech should be to decide the purpose of the speech. The selection of the main ideas should be the next step. After the selection of the main ideas, the supporting materials should be chosen. Examples of these materials are descriptions, comparisons, testimonies, and visual aids. Visual aids produce three valuable results: increased audience attention, initial understanding, and longer retention of ideas. These visuals should be large enough to be seen clearly by the audience. The selection of the main ideas and supporting materials completes the body of the speech.

The introduction of the speech usually has two parts, the opening, and the statement of purpose. In the beginning, the speaker catches the audience's attention and arouses interest in the subject. The statement of purpose tells precisely what the speaker intends to do in the speech.

A summary of the main ideas and specific purpose should be prepared. The outline is the final step of delivering an effective speech. A speaker usually delivers his talk directly from an outline or uses it as a basis for a written speech.

You can learn important things about a group by direct observation and conversation. Points in a speech often need strength to be completely believable. They sometimes need clarification, reinforcement, and proof.

You should have the ability to amplify speech ideas skillfully. To help keep an audience awake, alert and interested, the speaker should show their interest by their mood, manner, and voice. It would help if you talked using words, phrases, and sentences that will maintain attention. You should look at the audience, find a friendly face and occasionally speak directly to that person. It would help if you motivated the audience to arouse curiosity. It would be best if you learned to walk gracefully, stand erect, vary the pitch and volume of your voice to avoid delivering a boring speech. Each audience is a new experience. If you lose or gain one listener, it can make all the differences in being heard.

How To Age Gracefully and Successfully

◊ ◊ ◊ ◊ ◊ ◊

There are many ways of looking at old age and the new lifestyles it brings. Many people view this change with fear, while others keep referring to how great things were in the old days. When one begins to feel old, one should remember that age is a quality of the mind.

Many Americans past the age of sixty have experienced the dread of declining health, boredom, and a sense of uselessness. Old age, with all its complications, does not have to come as soon as it does. With the many incredible medical advances today, better nutrition, and more knowledge of how to take care of themselves, the elderly of today is healthier in body and mind than our ancestors were.

The ideas of aging differ with individuals. Many people today in their seventies and eighties sparkle with zest, are full of life, and enjoy whatever they do. We then have the other image of an older person as being confused, depressed, useless, and living in the past. Aging is nothing but a matter of the mind. Being youthful in spirit will contribute to physical strength and prolonged life. When many people have birthdays and reach sixty-five to seventy, they suddenly think they are old. A birthday does not determine whether someone is old or not. Many people in their seventies and eighties are young at heart, while others in their forties are old in appearance and their outlook on life.

The human body matures in about twenty-five to thirty years when the framework reaches its greatest size and strength. Most people, currently, begin to shrink. Others put on more weight. Those who shrink live longer because as the body shrinks, it reduces its number of cells. Some cells do not shrink but instead collect and store fatty substances in the arteries that interfere with the circulation and nourishment of the body, which eventually makes the heart pump harder and get more worn out. That can result in heart disease.

What we eat is vital in keeping the body in good running order. Proper nutrition is the best prevention for old age. Nutritious foods will provide and will help build up a resistance to diseases. Many older people eat less of the proper nutrients needed and often suffer from malnutrition. As they cut down on their activities, they will need fewer calories but should maintain a balanced diet.

Physical activities help a person look and feel better. Muscles, if not used, grow softly and flabby, losing their elasticity and strength. Activities involving leg muscles help maintain good circulation. In later years, it is crucial to refrain from suddenly taking on strenuous exercise. You should prepare your body for vigorous activities by warming up to it. As people age, it has been found that they need more sleep than before. However, this varies based upon the make-up of each person.

As the elderly grow older, they often experience frequent mild depressions. These episodes are often due to a lack of self-esteem, physical suffering, and a lower financial, professional, or social status. People often think that many older people become senile. That is not necessarily true. What often appears to be senility may be depression. However, actual cases of senility can result from some unwanted changes in a person's life, such as a forced retirement.

Many daily health habits may have to be changed for improved health in the elderly, such as smoking and drinking habits. An older person can do many things to ward off many diseases by keeping their weight down, watching cholesterol levels, and caring for persistent coughs and chest pains.

Accidents in older people are frequently due to falls, car mishaps, fires, and poisoning. That is mainly because their eyes are not as sharp as before, and they often miss steps, they do not smell smoke in time, have memory lapses, take overdoses of medicines, and often do not hear as well. To prevent accidents, they should not hurry. That usually causes a misstep or loss of balance.

Weather changes seem to affect the elderly more. Many deaths result from heat exhaustion and heat strokes. Some precautions you can take are never to over-exert yourself, bundle up in freezing weather, and dress suitably in hot weather.

Visual changes occur with advancing years. Most people become far-sighted. Reading glasses is a great help as well as bifocals. Two common eye diseases are cataracts and glaucoma. If not treated, they can cause blindness. An examination at least once a year and giving prompt attention to any signs of eye trouble is advisable.

Deafness increases vastly with age. That results from damage to nerve cells in the inner ear and to nerve fibers. An examination will indicate if the condition can be improved by treatment or surgery or helped by a hearing aid. If you wait too long, the return to better hearing is slower and sometimes impossible. To protect your hearing, you should keep your ears clean, let your doctor remove any excess wax, and at the first sign of ear pain or discharge, visit your doctor.

Good dental health is essential for nutrition. That affects what and how much you eat. Tooth decay is not due to aging as believed but often due to poor dietary habits. To prevent decay and save your teeth, you should see your dentist at least twice a year. As aging occurs, you should go to a doctor before an actual illness occurs and advise on food intake, exercise, rest, habits, recreation, family problems, etc. An annual thorough check-up is advisable.

Many more opportunities are open to older persons than ever before. The secret to successful aging is to keep living as full a life as possible. Your health in the years ahead can be just what you are willing to make of it. The elderly should learn to accept age for what it is, as well as those who share this time with them. Your prescription for aging should start today.

My Dad's Transitioning Journey

◊ ◊ ◊ ◊ ◊ ◊

I am the third child from a family of seven. As I can recall, I was told by my mother that I followed my dad around and wanted to go wherever he went with my overalls on and would become agitated if I could not go with him.

During my early years, I remember, most notably, my loving family. My parents were always there for all of us. We were then and remain today, a very tightly knitted family even though my parents are both deceased. Do we have sibling disagreements? Yes, of course, we do. Do we get angry and not speak to each other from time to time? Yes, of course, we do. But at the end of the day, we are one. My parents always engaged in family outings and activities that included each one of us participating. I especially remember the good times we shared at Christmas time. In early December, my mom would begin baking various cakes and pies for the holidays, making sure that her famous fruit cake was made for my brother, Lee's birthday on the 13th. My dad would light various cherry bombs, sparkles, and fireworks for us to throw and enjoy. He was a master at putting toys together for us.

On Christmas morning, the house would reek with the smell of oranges and tangerines that my parents would peel and eat during the late evening and toss the peelings in the hearth to be toasted by the fire and scent up the house. My mom would write each of us notes from Santa, supposedly, and place it in our own little "special spots."

As I grew older, my dad taught me to drive. He was enormously proud when I became the first of his children to obtain a driver's license. He also took me to purchase my first car and co-signed for my credit. I was always glad to let him drive my car when his vehicle was out of commission.

As time passed on, during my dating years, my boyfriend won my father's heart by tearing down, rebuilding, and racing his car, the "Roadrunner." Cars were exceedingly high on my dad's list because he enjoyed working on and fixing them as well.

My dad escorted me down the aisle on my wedding day to release me to my husband. I was the first of his children to have a church wedding, and he always mentioned how I did things differently.

I had never seen my dad sick a day in his life. He was always up early and out, making good use of his time for his family. One day my dad complained of being tired and out of breath after walking for truly short distances. He made an appointment with his doctor and, after many clinic visits, was told that he had a heart condition resulting from arteriosclerosis, a hardening of the arteries. He was told to stop smoking his Winston cigarettes and maintain a strict diet, which would reduce his intake of cholesterol and fat. He was a mild drinker, on weekends only, but was told to stop this as well.

He followed the doctor's orders as much as possible, but he was still a young man of only 50 years old. One cold dark day, my father suffered a mild stroke, which left him with paralysis of his right arm. Time after time, he continued to suffer from mild CVAs. These were more minor strokes, but each one left him with some facilitative condition. At this point, he was wheelchair-bound, his speech was not articulate, and his gait was very unsteady when trying to stand. We witnessed a happy-go-lucky man gradually go down in spirits and with little desire to gain his whole body back again. As time went on, I saw him give up a little each day. He was always happy to see us when we came around to visit. He was also incredibly sad when we were preparing to leave, and for the first time in my life, I would watch him cry and reach out to us as if we would not be back or he would not be around.

My father had numerous hospital stays, some short and some for prolonged periods. He underwent repetitions of tests after tests at the now-defunct Philadelphia General Hospital, owned and operated by the City of Philadelphia. Because I was employed at this facility, I was able to accompany him on many of the medical procedures and spend quality time with him daily. He was finally asked to submit to bypass surgery to rebuild collapsed arteries and to re-direct his blood flow around them. Each time, I am happy to admit that my father would bounce back, and despite the tedious procedures, remained very pleasant. He was a humble and easy-going person.

One Saturday morning, my father was complaining of not feeling well. I noticed that he was doing some very routine things backward. I saw him attempt to stir his hot coffee with his finger and unbutton his shirt that was just buttoned up. I knew something was wrong. He knew this too and reflected it by the worried look in his eyes. He was closely watched during the day and evening. On the next day, Sunday morning, we took my dad to Lankenau Hospital, Wynnewood, PA, and he was admitted. One unethical doctor told us that my dad would not live through the night. Doctors do not know everything, and this one was wrong. However, daddy was extremely sick this time but very much aware of his surroundings. He remained in the hospital for the remainder of the week. On the following Saturday, my brother, William and I were visiting our dad, standing at the foot of his bed, communicating with him by the blinking of his eyes, when a nurse came in and put what was supposed to be "Heparin," a blood thinner, in his IV. Just as she walked out of the room, I saw my dad go into a cold sweat and succumbed to a coma, right in front of our eyes. My brother and I summoned the nurse, who in turn contacted several doctors who worked on him and ultimately placed him on a heart monitor. My dad remained in a coma, so the family came and remained at the hospital around the clock. On Sunday night, when leaving for home, I truly felt that dad would not make it this time. He was now 61 years old and had suffered for so long.

On Monday morning at approximately 9:00 am, I was at work but called the hospital to see how my dad had endured during the night. I was told that he had a good night. I left my desk for no more than 15 minutes and when I returned, was told that the hospital had called me. When I returned the call, I was told that my dad has passed away. I now feel that he

had passed when I made the first call. I must have been in shock because I did not feel anything. I left work and drove myself to the hospital. When I looked upon my dad, he looked like he was sleeping with a peaceful look on his face. At this moment, I realized that my dad would not be around for me. I knew that a big chunk of me had just died with him. I also realized that his daughter had just lost her favorite dad.

I was not sure how my dad's death would affect me, but I do know that because of my teachings as a Christian, I have many religious beliefs. When we no longer exist on this earth, it should be a symbolic time for joy and not a time for sorrow. We should rejoice in knowing that if we have lived as Christians, here on earth, there will be a life afterlife, called immortality. I believe, like most Christians, in a continued and eternal life of a human being after the death of a body. This belief has formed a part of every religion. Some Jews believe that the good folks will someday return to life and share in God's kingdom. Many Christians have accepted this idea of resurrection and added the belief in continued spiritual existence in heaven. Christians also believe that people are rewarded or punished after they die, based on their way of life while living here on earth. With these beliefs bestowed upon me by my parents and pastors during my early life, I have grown to accept them as a way of life. I have also instilled these principles and beliefs in my children's Christian teachings.

Therefore, I suppose when my dad died, that I was faced with mixed emotions. My teachings had taught me that this is the norm and the way of the cross, but my love for my father and the knowledge that he would be physically removed from my presence was overwhelming.

We believe, as Christians, that in the land of "milk and honey," there will be no more pain. My dad had suffered for so long. If I could have wished anything, it would've been for him to rest in peace finally. I believe that my dad now rests in heaven and is finally free from sickness and pain.

The Sting of Death

◊ ◊ ◊ ◊ ◊ ◊

Medically speaking, death means the ending of vital functions, the end of life. One dies when the heart stops, and blood no longer circulates to bring oxygen and nourishment to body cells. All body cells do not die at once. For example, hair may continue to grow for several hours after death occurs. If the brain cells are complete without oxygen for only a few minutes, they can no longer regain their ability to function correctly. Cells in the skin and bones can live for several hours after death. I have learned that scientists have reported experiments in which life has been restored to dead human beings. Electrical shock applied to the heart can regain its pumping action when it has stopped.

I know that death is also a part of the processes of nature. Nature provides a cycle of experiences, including birth, growth, and reproduction. Death is the way the character ends the cycle. I have experienced that even though many people fear death, it can be calm and peaceful. Death has been named as one of the greatest enemies of humanity. It can occur from a decaying process like old age, but more commonly from accidents or some diseases. The life length of most living things is determined primarily by heredity. The percentage of older people in the world today is much more significant than ever before. That is a result of the decrease in the death rate of infants.

There are three standard modes of dying, and they begin in the lungs, heart, and brain. They are designated as suffocation, fainting, and comas. When a death occurs by suffocation, it starts at the lungs. That is when the functions of respiration have stopped. When the heart stops from loss of blood, death results from fainting. Death can also occur by a loss of nerve power and by starvation and thirst. When a death occurs by coma, it begins in the brain. That results in a loss of consciousness and is indicated by a stupor state, and breathing is accompanied by snoring. There are many forms of death, but one is no greater than the other. Most people do not seem to care about how they will die, but there is a fear for either method.

I have experienced that being of a religious nature makes dying easier for me. I believe God has given us life here on earth for a truly short time to enjoy and live to the fullest. I also think doctors and medicines have proven to be in vain when our time is near. On the other hand, death has been so apparent, but many people have refused to die, and Americans continue to wonder why.

Dr. Kubler-Ross describes the various stages of dying as denial and isolation, anger, bargaining, depression, and acceptance. Looking back in time and studying all cultures and people, we are impressed that death has always been distasteful to man and probably will always be.

Many mourners of death express grief in various ways. Many tend to blame themselves for the death of a loved one. The process of grief always includes some qualities of anger. These anger emotions are often disguised or repressed and prolong grief or show up in other ways. These are all signs of being human. Everyone should be allowed to ventilate their feelings, whether guilt, anger or plain sadness. Death is still a frightening experience, and the fear of death is a universal fear, even if we think we have mastered it. Denial is usually a temporary defense that is eventually replaced by partial acceptance. Unlike the denial stage, anger is exceedingly difficult to manage. The reason for this is the fact that anger is displaced in all directions and projected onto the environment at times, almost at random. Bargaining is an attempt to postpone the actual occurrence, and most are usually made with God and kept a secret. Depressions are well known to everybody. There are two types of depression; one is reactive depression, and the other is preparatory depression. They are different and should be dealt with differently. Shame and guilt are two factors that often accompany depression. Acceptance should not be mistaken for a happy stage. It is almost void of feelings, as if the pain has gone, the struggle is over, and it's time for the final rest before the long journey.

My Mama
A Virtuous Woman
Life Application Bible
(Proverbs Chapter 31: 1-31)

◊ ◊ ◊ ◊ ◊ ◊

Dear Mom,

Each time that I attempted to write about your life's journey and what you meant to me to be included in my book of cherished memories, I got writer's block, froze, and could not start. Perhaps, it is because I wanted to remember the good person you were and envision you as still being here with me, but just sleeping in your Heavenly home. So, I decided to dedicate this chapter of scripture to you because it is so befitting for who you were. I thank God for you, all that you taught me, and the love you shared. I will never forget you and will always cherish your sweet memory. When Gabriel blows the horn, I will see you in the rapture, the meeting in the air. Tell dad I will see him too.

Your Loving Daughter,
Jackie

These are the sayings of King Lemuel, an oracle that his mother taught him:

O my son, of my womb, O son of my promises, do not spend your strength on women, on those who ruin kings. And it is not for kings, O Lemuel, to guzzle wine. Rulers should not crave liquor. For if they drink, they may forget their duties and be unable to give justice to those who are oppressed. Alcohol is for the dying, and wine for those in deep depression. Let them drink to forget their poverty and remember their troubles no more. Speak up for those who cannot speak for themselves; ensure justice for those who are perishing. Yes, speak up for the poor and helpless, and see that they get justice. Who can find a virtuous and capable wife? She is worth more than precious rubies. Her husband can trust her, and she will greatly enrich his life. She will not hinder him but help him all her life. She finds wool and flax and busily spins it. She is like a merchant's ship; she brings her food from afar. She gets up before dawn to prepare breakfast for her household and plans the day's work for her servant girls. She inspects a field and buys it; with her earnings, she plants a vineyard. She is energetic and strong, a hard worker. She watches for bargains; her lights burn late into the night. Her hands are busy spinning thread, her fingers twisting fiber. She extends a helping hand to the poor and opens her arms to the needy. She has no fear of winter for her household because all of them have warm clothes. She quilts her bedspreads. She dresses like royalty in gowns of the finest cloth. Her husband is well known, for he sits in the council meeting with the other civic leaders. She makes belted linen garments and sashes to sell to the merchants. She is clothed with strength and dignity, and she laughs with no fear of the future. When she speaks, her words are wise, and kindness is the rule when she gives instructions. She carefully watches all that goes on in her household and does not have to bear the consequences of laziness. Her children stand and bless her. Her husband praises her." There are many virtuous and capable women in the world, but you surpass them all!" Charm is deceptive, and beauty does not last, but a woman who fears the Lord will be greatly praised. Reward her for all she has done. Let her deeds publicly declare her praise.

Biography

Jacqueline McNeil-Henry was born October 31, 1948, in the Mule Town of Pamplico, South Carolina, to the late William Lawrence McNeil, Sr. and Frances Mae Myers McNeil. Jackie, as she is affectionately called, is the 3rd child of seven siblings born from this marital union. Seeking greater opportunities, Jackie's parents relocated the family from South Carolina to Philadelphia in 1962.

Jackie is the mother of Rashid Tyrone Henry and Shatyra Blondell Henry. She is the immensely proud mom-mom to her only grandchild, Jalen Rashid Henry. Her children are her every heartbeat. She proudly accepts being called mom by so many others, near and far.

Jackie attained her educational and employment endeavors in Philadelphia. After an amazingly successful career, she retired from City Government in 2007, after 41 years of dedicated service. Following her retirement, Jackie provided executive consulting services to her church, Resurrection Baptist. In 2015, she purchased a home in Atlanta, Georgia, where she relocated and currently resides.

On April 13, 2021, Jackie, unfortunately, lost her furry friend, Angel Pearl, who had been her constant companion and friend for 16 years. This, of course, left a tremendous void in Jackie's life, so the idea occurred to her that writing a book would be a fulfilling project for her to pursue in the absence of her furry friend. So, she marveled at the idea, got out her pen and paper, put on her cap of reflections, and began writing this project to share with others.

Some of Jackie's favorite past times are singing, photography, browsing in antique and thrift shops, travel, and doting on her children and grandson. She thanks God for the journey.

www.ingramcontent.com/pod-product-compliance
Lightning Source LLC
Chambersburg PA
CBHW071422070526
44578CB00003B/665